Light and Dark

A collection of poems
By
Kevin Heads

I dedicate this book of poetry to my Mother
Edna May Heads

'Forever the light in my Darkness,'

A FEW WORDS FROM THE AUTHOR:

In this book, you will find a selection of poems out of almost five hundred I have written to date. I have chosen them with care and consideration and hope you find my selections interesting, thought provoking and a little different from other poetry books you have read.

Because I write poems on a multitude of subjects, I wanted this to be reflected in this book. So I have sectioned them according to topic. You can read them in whatever order you like according to your mood. However, one day you will have to read the Dark Side ☺

My style is simplistic, but within these words, I hope you will find something that appeals and makes you pause for thought, reflect on life and maybe even laugh a little. There is something for everyone.

When I write, I try to place myself in the topic's heart. I virtually live the moment; I see it, hear it, and most of all, feel the emotions within the narrative. Almost like watching a movie.

I hope this comes across in my poetry and that you enjoy reading these poems as much as I have writing them.

I dedicated this book to my mother because I had never written a single word of poetry in my life until my mother decided it was time to leave this world for the next.

Poetry is good for the soul and in the words of my favourite poet…

'I was never really insane except upon occasions when my heart was touched.' Edgar Allan Poe.

'Nevermore,'

ACKNOWLEDGMENTS

Love and support are two of the greatest gifts anyone can receive from another human being. Although this book I dedicated to my mother, it would never have been written if it hadn't been for my wife.

She is my backbone, her love and compassion are infinite, and I thank her with all my heart for all her support throughout our life together. She is my soul mate.

I would also like to thank my dad, who has always been there for me, and has so much belief in my creative endeavours. The opening poem is his favourite and I can't think of a better one to start with.

I would like to thank all my friends, especially those on Facebook, who never fail to comment on the poems I post online. You're all so supportive, and look, I have finally done what you have been nagging me to do for years.

Finally, and not least, there is one special poem in this book I would like to dedicate to my biggest fans, Caelan and Melissa Speed.

Death of a King was one of my earliest poems and I know it is their favourite.

CONTENTS

Historical

OH HOW I LOVED THE BEACH.

Oh, how I loved the beach when I was young,

A striped deck chair where my jumper hung.

Yet now I stand on blood-soaked sand,

A uniformed man with a gun in his hand.

My sister laughed as I splashed her face.

Returned in kind a loving embrace.

As my brothers in arms fall to the ground,

Some still alive but many downed.

Hot summer sun and lemonade,

Fond memories of the games we played.

Where bullets sing and missiles soar,

Another falls, then many more.

I feel the breeze that strokes my hair,

A life so happy without a care.

Blue no more the sky turns black,

We try once more, our last attack.

The gulls cry as my kite flies high.

Thoughts fade of my last goodbye.

To those I love, there and here,

One more step to face the fear.

And now I sit near cliffs so white,

Where planes once flew, every day, every night.

A survivor unscathed from the acts of war,

Yet still they are dying and I ask what for.

Through poppy fields the sea's now red,

Remembrance of my friends long dead.

A silent salute for those out of reach,

Oh dear, how I used to love this beach.

DEATH OF A KING

How laboured my heart beats,

As I survey the remnants of my regal seat.

Lost is my crown on blood-soaked fields,

No horse to ride, no sword to wield.

So many lost who loved me so,

Their souls blown away as the north wind blows.

And as I rest against this hollow tree,

I watch royal blood as it flows from me.

The sky darkens as the heavens cry,

Rain dulled thuds make the ravens fly.
A wanderer with staff passes me by,

With a bearded face and a single eye.

An eerie silence settles on the battleground.

Like a blanketed mist that smothers all sound.

The wanderer beckons I'm urged to follow,

To a land of joy far away from this sorrow.

A last glance at my weeping tree,

Whose branches hang low to cradle me.

As the raven squawks, the blackbird sings.

Lost is the kingdom dead is my King.

GODDESS WITH THE PALE GREEN EYES

Walls of men cross my path,

Signal warnings of an aftermath.

Doubt extinguished confidence reigns,

As a howling roar starts our blood letting games.

A prayer offered, a soul's demise,

A gift to my Goddess with the pale green eyes.

Teeth gritted, effort bold,

I fight for the honour and a story told.

Red mist that stings my eyes,

As a blade slashes deep against my thigh.

It's just a scratch from a man so tall,

So I cut him down, and now he is small.

The ring of swords and clash of shields,

Skin from bone lightly peeled.

Every sinew stretched and strained,

By men who fight, a few remain.

Then all at once quiet ensues,

Battle torn flags and crows that muse.

As survivors float away like ghosts,

And the winners raise a victory toast.

To the Goddess with the pale green eyes,

Who casts her magic and weaves her lies,

A blessed gift she gave this day,

Permission to live an enemy to slay.

With darkness comes the moans of death,

Smoke filled fields from a dragon's breath.

Screams of mercy as the reaper creeps,

With a promise of hope and eternal sleep.

In Memory of the Battle of Towton 1461

TWO ROSES

Men in armour, courageous and bold,

Stood in the snow and shivered with cold.

Poleaxe in hand, held firm in a glove,

Ready to die for the King that they loved.

Cock Beck runs fast, swollen with hail,

They fight to the death, refusing to fail.

But many have fallen, brutally dead.

As the trees weep with sorrow, and the river runs red

Arrows fly, goose feathered rain.

As they punctured armour, men screamed out in pain.

When one cloud breaks, another one falls.

And the reaper screams out his murderous call.

Two roses in a field, one red, one white.

Armed with thorns, they battle, they fight.

Each believing their cause is just,

But as each petal falls, it crumbles to dust.

I stand here and listen. There is no sound,

No battle cries, no snow on the ground.

The land weeps for souls long lost.

The ones who fought and died in the frost.

Beauty now hides the scars of war,

No bridge of bodies on the rivers floor.

Just peace and quiet and birds in flight,

Who sing of the roses, one red and one white.

BOOTS ON THE GROUND

Souls bend as boots hit the ground,

A hail of bullets and a wall of sound.

I dive behind a sandy mound,

Then turn and look, there's no one around.

Earth shattering the smoke clears,

My friends all gone in a single tear.

How can this be when I stood so near,

When our boots hit the ground and we shared the fear.

Pinned down, I hold my hat,

The guns blaze on as the planes attack.

Afraid to move and face the flak,

I cower and shake like a frightened cat.

Whispers urge me to run the gun,

Push through the darkness and find the sun.

Show your heels till the battles won,

Till the sand is dry and the boots are hung.

Worn away from marching South,

Laces snapped the tongues hang out.

Lost souls the dead can't shout,

And their boots no longer march about.

Written about The Osberg Viking boat burial

A BUCKET OF APPLES

When I used to sail to foreign lands,

There was always an apple in my hand.

Red and delicious, succulently sweet,

A taste of home, a humble treat.

I gave one to a King, instead of gold.

Who mocked my gift, or so I was told.

Yet apples come from a tree of life,

A precious gem for his Danish wife.

So beautiful with her small red cheeks.

Long dark hair with auburn streaks.

Her nakedness always made me sigh,

For she was a goddess and the apple of my eye.

I admit it's true; I stole her away,

Love is a dangerous game we must play.

Within the heart, the seeds will grow,

Branches above and roots below.

I brought her home to live her life.

A better place for my Danish wife.

Surrounded by an orchard of trees,

Kissed by the rain and the mountain breeze.

And when she died, her soul to float,

I laid her gently on my sailing boat.

Beneath the trees where sunlight dapples,

Is my queen, my love and a bucket full of apples.

MARY

This room, this cell, it haunts me.

Whispering walls, the reaper taunts me.

I sit alone with pen and ink,

My life's reflection, a time to think.

I asked not for status. I was born a queen.

A regal pawn, a threat, it seems.

Treason my crime, or so they said.

And I will die by the axe that severs my head.

Cold is the pen in my shaking hand,

To write my thoughts to a foreign land.

Not long to go, my King, my friend,

The final chapter of my life to end.

I pray to my God, my love I give.

And through my son my soul will live,

I will lose my crown but gain another,

She may be a queen, but I am a mother.

Time is torturous, so slow it flows.

Like a blood filled river to the highlands it goes.

My time is spent as the door unlocks.

But history will remember the Queen of Scots.

THE WANDERER

My world is empty. Now you are gone.

Far beyond the snow-capped hills.

Where the river screams in angry fluidity

Slaughtered as I slept in peace and tranquility.

My death averted, I sit alone.

Flames flicker, teasing the faces of my wife and child.

Tears sizzle in red hot sorrow,

I yearn to sleep before the 'morrow.

In my dreams, I'm truly blessed,

No more to suffer in morbid solitude.

Laughter rains in joyful showers,

My guilt subdued in these darkened hours.

Yet as it must, the morning breaks.

And I wander once more in this savage land.

Yearning to fight, to seek revenge,

To slay the mighty, my heart avenged.

But the weight of loss is a heavy burden,

It stains my soul, a hollow black.

Mired within a torture pit,

My mind, in chains of silence, sits.

Days, weeks, months and years,

I wander far on land and sea.

A battered shield, a bloodstained blade,

A trail of death I've carefully laid.

Every kill brings me closer to you,

Every battle cry is my song of love.

And on the day I lie in death,

I will utter your names with my final breath.

TEUTOBURG FOREST

The trees creak their wagging tale,

Where spears bite hard and swords impale.

Screams echo in this forest land,

A place of death where victory stands.

Scattered corpses, pools of red,

Guts and gore and dispatched heads.

Ravens pluck the fallen eyes,

As the wolves gather close, to howl and cry.

Three golden eagles cast asunder,

A barbarian storm of light and thunder.

Blood teared rain stains the battleground,

Where the moans of the dying are the only sounds.

And as darkness crawls, the branches crack,

The clouds pull apart as the sky turns black.

Silence descends with a shivering call,

And blankets the ground where the Romans fall.

BEBBANBURG

Ripples of sand on a time soaked beach,

Reaching out for the castle's keep.

Swords and shields and battle sounds,

From ghostly warriors, who stood their ground.

Blood washed beach, the tide ferocious,

Waves carry ships, the foe approaches.

But this is Bebbanburg, on cliffs so steep.

A place to die and gods to meet.

Dark clouds gather and mist rolls in,

To muffle the screams from the arrows within.

Never to fall, always to stand,

The fortress that guards Northumberland.

Memory pools of crabs and worms,

Pick the bones as the ocean turns.

Sweeping away the history web,

To leave the graves of ripples bled.

Quiet now the palisade,

As the visitors leave and the daylight fades.

Yet the gulls still scream a battle call,

For the men that died at the castle walls.

Ripples mark the passage of time,

The hammer strikes and the church bells chime.

Carried across a bay of sand,

To Bebbanburg castle, long may it stand.

The Natural World

YESTERDAY WE WERE FOUR

Yesterday we were four,

Happily wandering the Savannah floor.

Flicking dust near a watering hole,

Where we danced and pranced, jumped and rolled.

Happy, like cranes in flight,

We sprayed the water till the day turned night.

Then we slept in a group, our snoring trunks,

Dreaming peacefully in our sand filled bunks.

My father gasped as the shot rang out,

From dreams to death, there was never a doubt.

My mother ran, calling us near.

But I stood firm, as my eyes formed a tear.

Too small to pose a viable threat,

Or hang as a trophy, not big enough yet.

No glorious tusks, my feet too small,

I need to be bigger to sit on their wall.

So I stand and watch as they cut and tear,

Piece by piece, layer by layer.

Hooting and cheering, they carry him off.

As one turns to whisper, so sorry for your loss.

I stroke what's left of his murdered hide,

He was kind and gentle, forever at my side.

Bereft, I feel, as the others return,

The pain inside is such a torturous burn.

Elephants never forget, they say,

I will live with this horror, every hour, every day.

Traumatised mind of a damaged daughter,

Who witnessed a crime, a murder, a slaughter.

RAIN

I love the sound of rain,

As it pits and pats,

Spits and spats,

Tapping, rapping on my windowpane.

Wind driven, a crowd of wet,

Rushing, pushing,

Gushing, slushing,

Moving, grooving no time to set.

Icy cold, relief from the heat,

Shiver, quiver,

Surging river,

Carried on sheets of air to greet.

Then frozen, as the temperature falls,

Flakes and shakes,

Snowballs make,

Clear to white as winter calls.

Sun kissed, a melting pot,

Dripping, slipping,

Lack of gripping,

Evaporate, as the rain gets hot.

Gone now in a sky so blue,

Hiding, riding,

Convection gliding,

No clouds of rain to spoil the view.

LIGHT

Sunlight, radiant in all its glory,

A universal story of bright desire,

Shining, climbing, refining the shadows that creep away from

outstretched rays of the days of light.

A sight, a wonderful sight,

So glowing, flowing, a fiery dragon with breath warming,

Utters a warning as it slips below the earth's curve.

Light dimming, horizon skimming,

Swimming in a sea of twinkling stars.

Till drowned, the sound lapping, seagulls flapping,

Children napping, the day is done.

Moonlight, white in the night, what a cratered delight,

I stare at the wondrous sight, so pure, lily white against the velvet

sky.

I sigh, I cry, I wonder why I feel such madness in her glorious show,

Bathed, swathed, in layers of luminous glow, like snow, there is an

icy chill that spills, yet still I can see in the dark.

Light in the night, the owl takes flight,

What a sight, such pure delight

Firelight bright, sparks ignite,

Like a kite carried on a breeze so slight.

A false light, orange embers, flicked, licked, pricked with red,

Crackling, cackling, like burning witches,

Making wishes, casting spells.

As bells ring, a blackbird sings,

To greet the dawn, a new day brings.

Daylight, a chorus of hope filled songs,

Singing, ringing, brightness bringing,

Golden colours to greet the day.

Children play in the morning dew,

As black turns blue, a spider's silver web drips sips of watery wine,

So fine, sublime, brightness divine,

Let the glorious light forever shine.

THE WILDS OF WANNIE

Feel the North wind blow,

A light dusting of freezing snow.

Slippery steps, lightly tread,

Upon the Wilds of Wannie.

Spring flowers bloom,

Bursting colour that devours the gloom.

As birds chirp their mating call,

Upon the Wilds of Wannie.

A blazing summer sun,

A place of warmth for deer to run.

As young hawks learn to hover and hunt,

Upon the Wilds of Wannie.

Then the trees turn red,

Dropping leaves, they prepare for bed.

As the crows call a winter's warning,

Upon the Wilds of Wannie.

And so full circle I gather my sheep,

Before the snow lies crispy and deep.

A winter's soup by a blazing fire,

How I love the Wilds of Wannie.

THE STORM

In the heat of summer, blue skies turn dark.

The birds fall silent, as a small dog barks.

A cooling breeze spikes the humid air,

It crackles a laugh as we offer a prayer.

Like ghouls, the clouds creep and crawl.

Wispy fingers, large and small.

Spears of light pierce the gloom.

A beast is born from its swirling womb.

Rain paints like the artist's brush,

A rainbow vista, a pigment crush.

Reflected greys in teardrop eyes,

A masterful piece on canvas lies.

Out at sea, the waves grow tall,

Like a mountain range, they rise and fall.

Run to port, the captain calls.

Safe behind the harbour walls.

Lightning arcs and thunder cracks,

Within the grey, throughout the blacks.

The ground thumps beneath our feet,

As the Gods rearrange their tables and seats.

Then the rain subsides, and the lightning dies,

A final rumble to say goodbye.

A solemn silence as fissures so bright,

Disperse the dark return the light.

A moment of silence, a mark of respect.

A place to consider, connect, or reflect.

As the sun shines, the air grows warm.

And in retrospect, I yearn for the storm.

TSUNAMI

There were so many birds that day,

Filling the sky and flying away.

Shrill cries echoed along the beach.

Higher ground and safety to reach.

I watched them and felt their fear.

That something was creeping, drawing near.

It was strange, a quiet atmosphere,

Then I noticed the ocean had disappeared.

Frozen in a statue state,

I didn't run I elected to wait.

Till the white tipped stallions turned to the shore,

They were coming in fast I froze no more

My heart raced the adrenaline seared,

Urging me forward as the stampede neared.

Hands of wind pushing me harder,

As the beach got smaller and the wave got larger.

There was no escape,

No chance or fortune, no twist of fate.

So I faced my destiny and gasped in awe,

At nature's power, on the sand filled floor.

So many birds in the sky that day,

Warning me to leave, but instead I stayed.

Hesitating just a moment too long,

Wondering where the ocean had gone

FIRE

It makes my nose twitch,

An unreachable itch that makes my senses scream.

Danger, fear, lets run my dear,

Far from peril away from here.

It's far off for now, but it crackles with speed.

A demon freed, take heed my dear,

For its touch will sear sizzling flesh,

For those who linger, such a terrible death.

Greyness weaves through trees and bush,

Let's rush, for grey is a choking shade.

Be afraid, so afraid, my dear.

Closer now, it's drawing near.

Pain filled heat, flames to meet.

If your pace slows, you will wither and die.

Don't dither in the face of the burning wall,

For there's no escape if you stumble and fall.

The roar rises like a crescendo of doom.

A panic filled concerto blares through the gloom.

The instruments of death with breath that kills,

If you're slow of foot, or you 're standing still.

Alas, I can run no more, my dear.

My pace slows, my limbs ache,

My fate is sealed. I stand and wait.

For smoke filled lungs to asphyxiate.

Yet in that moment, the rain falls,

The Gods call to save our souls.

In swirls and curls, the grey retreats

My heart slows down to a resting beat.

The roar of the fire now spits and spats.

The temperature falls on the thermostat.

Sizzling with hate, its flames fall flat,

Whilst mocking the destruction of our habitat.

LIFE

Look for me and you will find me there,

Under every rock, in sea and in air.

I scuttle, I swim, I can crawl and walk,

Be silent or sing, I can shout and talk.

Yes, within all things I like to reside,

In a body or shell, I will lurk or hide.

Watching, exploring and making love,

I'm a shark, I'm a wolf, I'm a peaceful dove.

I mean no harm yet survive I must,

In polar ice or sands of dust.

I will kill and maim, save and heal,

From time to time, I will even steal.

Because to live is truly a gift from the stars,

Complexity wrapped in a stardust bar.

A quasar of light, a circle of dark,

Particles mixed to make a bright spark.

And like a sculpture from an artist's knife,

Nature carves the signs of life

Perfect lines and forms so grand

Life in the skies, in the seas and on land.

RIVER OUSE

You meander curling like a viper,

Slow when the tide is turning.

No rush, for your majesty is graceful under a moonlit sky.

Yet flooded so dangerous,

Slithering fast past field and tree.

Like a sea, you smother and drown,

Across the land, through village and town.

I listen and watch your pattern glisten.

Twinkling ripples as you slip silently by.

Hardly noticed, just a trickle,

so little it barely licks my elderly ears.

What tales you tell,

The things you've seen,

I can but dream of the longboats carried on your watery back.

Gone now, but you remain,

Slinking, sliding, still the same.

Three swans swimming, a sign from a God,

To build a church for all to share.

You were there when the first stones were laid.

Foundations turned to grandeur,

Kings born of Queens, such a grand parade.

Bear witness, for the tide is turning towards the sea,

And I watch in awe as you swim from me.

Low tide, fish hiding in the rocks and pools,

Resting for it is too fast to swim.

Crows watch from perches high,

As the sun gleams bright in a winter's sky.

They caw and croak, their feathers black,

Echoing omens from the chimney stacks.

But I do not fear,

For I know you must return,

Nature demands it, and God commands it.

So I will sit and wait till you whisper once more.

Till the hiss of the viper creeps and crawls,

Your wide expanses and waterfalls,

Like watery veins, some large, some small.

Such power,

Your beauty deep like a Yorkshire flower,

White your rose with petals so bright,

Your elegant light reflected, twinkling within the gentle waves.

Lost now, the boats that carried the coal and grain,

So sad the memory, yet you remain.

Still the same,

The Yorkshire River with a Celtic name.

TREES

How low the Willow weeps,

Kissing the earth in sweet sorry.

Whispering on a summer's breeze,

That a happier day may come tomorrow.

How tall the Oak stretching skywards,

Searching the heavens for love and hope.

Creaking branches that bow and bend,

As children swing, from a tethered rope.

The Beech with its rounded head,

So tall and wide, sublime in elegance.

A coat so dark with sleeves of green,

I marvel at its glorious reverence.

The Birch, silvery and slender,

Stretches high to reach the clouds.

A gleaming family like soldiers stand,

Their feet planted, their trunks unbowed.

Ash, so graceful, a beloved tree,

With little black buds and clusters of seeds.

That fall and spin on wings so slim,

To nourish the Earth and forests feed.

So majestic of all the trees,

With layers of branches and foliage green.

Needles and cones, a stately mix,

The Cedar paints a stunning scene.

Oh, how wondrous is the world of trees,

A spiritual haven that soothes our mind.

To hear their chatter and smell their scent,

Be grateful for the gifts they leave behind.

THE JOURNEY

White tipped torrents of frantic thought,

Race the rapids, bubbling and fraught.

Desperate salmon leap and strain,

To higher ground, to spawn again.

Channels and grooves cut deep in stone.

A place to sit, or stand-alone.

Flickering lights through branches gleam,

Flashes of light on a summer's stream.

Racing rapids like giggling girls,

Young and loud with hair that curls.

Dancing swirling to a rhyme extreme,

A place of hope for youthful dreams.

Slower now with width and depth,

Pulled by lunar madness crept.

Turning in an arc so bold,

The waters deep and icy cold.

Lapping on the harbour walls,

Run with the wind the ocean calls.

Till lovers meet on sands of old,

And within their arms, the waters fold.

A WONDROUS LIFE

A life is such a wondrous thing,

To see the world, to hear it sing.

To bathe in light, the cosmos brings,

Day and night, a constant spin.

To smell the sea, to feel its chill,

To float upon is such a thrill.

To lie upon a grassy hill,

When the sun is warm, and the wind is still.

To hear the birds their varied song,

Whose coloured feathers are short and long.

Cast them high to glide and soar,

Above the fields and forest floor.

To see the colours, a canvas bold,

A rose so red, a field of gold.

A butterfly so fragile, to gently hold.

As the oak watches on, with eyes so old.

Taste the honey, nectar sweet,

Or the sugary treat of cane or beet.

Feel the soil beneath our feet,

Winter cold or summer heat.

Time is short upon this earth,

We start to die from our day of birth.

So fill the days with joy and mirth.

And indulge yourself for all your worth.

LOOK AWAY

It's easy to avert one's eyes from proof,

To ignore the facts, deflect the truth.

Refuse to hear the fear of those,

Who are watching the planet decompose.

Ice melting in a warming sea,

Forests shrinking, tree-by-tree.

Extinction nibbling, in sea and on land,

Picked and plucked for greedy hands.

Temperatures rising, as eyes stay shut,

The fires still burn and the saws still cut.

The plastic floats on a turning tide,

We can't escape, no place to hide.

Time keeps ticking on the doomsday clock,

It won't slow down or be forced to stop.

Little by little, piece by piece,

Records broken on the press release.

What a legacy we shouldn't be proud,

Chocked to death by our climate cloud.

Suffer the children for averting our eyes,

Ignoring the truth and embracing the lies.

DROPLET

I can see my world reflected in your mirror like tears.

As you hang, ready to fall, a drop of perfection, a watery ball.

I hold out my hand as you finally drip, a spit of rain that erupts into a

million fragments of liquid shrapnel.

Then, like magic, you pool in my cradling hand,

Till, like a fool, I wipe you away.

Now there's a stain, dark and damp where you now lay,

Devoured by the fabric, worn and frayed.

I watch, amazed as you slowly disappear, millimetre by millimetre

you leave my sleeve,

Like a soul ascending, you rise and leave.

I look for you but you 're not there. Your twinkling beauty lost.

Tossed into a sea of a warming breeze that lifts you high in the cloud

filled sky.

Sailing there on pillows of twisting air, I send my eyes to find you

there.

A chilly warning makes my skin pop as I shiver under a darkening

sphere.

Creeping closer, a whip-like crack punctures the pillowed bosom

that holds you near,

I wait with anticipation for the liquid parcel of precipitation.

Falling earthwards with gathering pace,

I spread my arms and raise my face.

Oblivious to the time and place,

Your beauty, your grace, your wet embrace.

Humour

IS THE WORLD FLAT?

I read a theory that the world was flat,

Not round like a ball, but level like a mat.

Water can't flow upwards, I heard them say.

As the seas would slide off in a slippery way.

Straight as an arrow, not curved or bowed,

The horizon stretches outward like a newly laid road.

The argument for flatness is valid and strong,

Could it be that science has got it all wrong?

Oh the confusion, Ive had years of teaching,

Biology and physics a knowledge far reaching.

Yet here we are now with doubt asunder,

Is it a lie? Or a catastrophic blunder?

Blue was this sphere I always believed,

It's presented in pictures and books that I read.

Maybe triangular, rectangle or cubed,

As I search wikipedia, google and you tube.

The truth must be out there, the X files say.

A cross on my window that won't fade away.

I will ask the Alien from across the street,

With the black oval eyes and long pointed feet.

He's been up to the heavens, or so he proclaims.

But prefers the Earth for its video games.

He's toured the galaxy and seen it all.

Smiling, he whispers, Its round like a ball.

ORANGE GLOW

There's so many orange faces,

From home towns to far-off places.

Cheeks blossoming with an amber hue,

Buy the make-up and join the queue.

Matched with the middle traffic light,

A scary look, such a dreadful sight.

Heads like carrots with curly lashes,

Speckled necks with pure white patches.

This is no tangerine dream,

It is a nightmare causing ocherous screams.

Terrifying monsters that shine at night,

Caught in the headlights, a reflective fright.

It isn't pretty, it's not even cute,

To have a face like a citrus fruit.

You don't see lemon, grapefruit or lime,

So why do you think mandarins fine?

It gathers in pools when you smile or frown.

Thick like a paint from Dulux or Crown.

It's not a good look, trust me, I know,

Our eyes are offended by your clementine glow.

OVER INDULGENCE

Oh, I feel like a beached whale,

So much food I can hardly inhale.

That final morsel such a delicate slice,

Wrapped in bacon so deliciously nice.

Three glasses of wine to wash it all down,

Followed by ice cream, a chocolate brown.

A wafer or two for added delight,

Pop goes a button, a frightening sight.

I feel quite sick if the truth be told,

But I can't resist a lager so cold.

With icy droplets and bubbling froth,

Such a glorious, golden, fermented broth.

Three pints later, my heads in a spin,

I rush to the toilet but can't get in.

My gut is complaining its ready to blow,

I can wait, says my head, but my stomach says no.

I'm banned from that restaurant,

No more to indulge.

After losing the contents of my decadent bulge.

I lowered my head, made a hasty retreat,

A night to forget at Bon appétit.

THE MANAPAUSE

I think I'm suffering the manopause,

Not enough testosterone could be the cause.

I'm middle-aged, just like my wife,

But there's no medication for my change of life.

No HRT to help with my moods,

No plastic surgery to reduce my boobs.

My belly grows an inch by the day,

I want to be young and push aging away.

I'm depressed, as my chubby cheeks puff out air,

My beard is grey and my heads lacking hair.

I have all the symptoms of a midlife crisis,

Looking for remedies at exorbitant prices.

But nothing works. My sex drive stutters,

It's fading away as it limps through the gutters.

From a tall tower to a wet damp tent,

My mind is willing, but my ardour is spent.

And so I write to keep me sane,

Helping me through this manopause pain.

Capturing all in chapter and verse,

To relieve the symptoms of a maturing curse.

ALIEN GIRLFRIEND

I saw a UFO the other day,

It hovered, then arced and flew away.

There was no sound, no gentle hum.

As it flew through the clouds, I turned to run.

Looking back, I caused the collision,

With a goddess so bright, an alien vision.

Smiling eyes, so dark with allure,

She looked so innocent, fragile, and pure.

Come she said, inside my mind,

No spoken word or chat up line.

Just matter of fact, so off we went,

To a field near the woods and a pop up tent.

There we lay for a week and a day,

Till the craft came back and whisked her away.

Lost and sad, I ventured home,

Cursing the fact she had left me alone

And now at night I search the sky,

Confused, I consider the reasons why.

An alien would want a one week stand,

On a hostile world, in a foreign land.

I pray one day that she returns,

To seek me out for my heartache burns.

For love is universal and earth girls are dull,

And my alien girlfriend was so easy to pull.

CABBAGE

What is this upon my plate?

Shredded sliced, green leaves of hate.

Hidden within my potatoes and peas,

It lies in wait to terrorize me.

It tastes like metal, a poisonous lead,

That will make me ill and send me to bed.

To eat it would cause me a cataclysm,

An atomic attack on my digestive system.

I tenderly push it away from the rest.

From the carrots, the meat, the things that taste best.

For to taint perfection with this green curly leaf,

Would be a deed so sinful and an insult to beef.

Don't force me to eat this brassica demon,

It's an unnecessary evil beyond rhyme or reason.

Let me eat pizza, fish fingers, or crisps.

Who cares if it puts a few pounds on my hips.

It's an evil weapon of gut destruction,

Whose fallout is rancid and totally disgusting.

It will kill you slowly as it clears out the room,

Where you will die all alone from cabbagy fumes.

Whether white or red, the result is the same.

So save your apologies as you're to blame.

It's a dietary disaster, it's wicked and savage,

And I, for one, will not eat this cabbage.

CHRISTMAS JUMPERS

Nobody should wear a Christmas jumper,

It should be ripped from the body and cast asunder.

It's not a good look, it's pathetically sad,

They're tacky and cheap, and fashionably bad.

A woolen monstrosity, it makes me weep,

A textile nightmare that's insulting to sheep.

A garment for the mad, the fool, and dimwitted,

Poorly made and unevenly knitted.

When three wise men turned up at the barn,

There was frankincense, myrrh, no mention of yarn.

A newborn king was in swaddling clothes.

Not santa suited baby grows.

And lets not forget the mohair trees,

It's enough to bring a goat to its knees.

Such luster and shine, a must for the rich,

I hope they scratch, irritate, and itch.

And finally, the awful cardigan of cheer,

For overweight men who smoke and drink beer.

With baubled buttons that fasten too tight,

Stretched across bellies, they pop and take flight.

Please save me from this festive gloom,

Burn all the jumpers and break all the looms.

Just wear the clothes that fit you the best,

And give my eyes a Yuletide rest.

VIRTUALLY REAL

Thank God for games, in my time of need,

From Call of Duty to Assassin's Creed.

They keep me busy and mentally sane,

I have an excuse, a virus to blame.

You should see my new car, it's fast and sleek,

As I tear around the virtual streets.

There's no better driver. I'm a racing pro.

King of the circuit in Gran Turismo

I explore Uncharted, looking for gold,

Following clues on a map that I hold.

Sailing the seas on a pirate ship,

Chased by villains, what a dangerous trip.

Too many zombies out on the street,

So I run and hide from the monsters I meet.

Through empty streets, I creep and crawl,

Self-isolating is a sensible call.

I have fought a war in trenches of mud,

Stepped over bodies covered in blood.

Taking orders, a mission revealed,

Blowing up the tanks on the Battlefield.

Storm troopers surround my base,

A mighty army I have to face.

So I ask my cousin to help me fight,

The odds are better with two Jedi knights.

Modern Warfare is hard and tough,

Gathering weapons and valuable stuff.

Stay alive and save yourself,

For others will kill you and steal all your wealth.

My wife squeals we have no bread,

It fills me with terror, horror and dread.

For now, I must face my deadliest foe,

Out into the real, to Tesco's I go.

ENDGAME

I loved Spiderman when I was a kid,

I tried to copy the things he did.

A broken arm and battered head,

I thought I would be the Hulk instead.

Crayola green made me mad,

I tore my shirt to be big and bad.

I climbed on cars and punched the ground.

Not the best idea I found.

So my parents bought me an Ironman suit,

It wasn't metal, but I looked really cute.

I tried to fly from the garden shed,

A nine-foot drop, Ironman dead.

I found a hammer, so Thor was next.

I threw it hard at my best friend's chest.

He fell gasping, his face went red,

I aimed for his head but hit ribs instead.

Captain America, the ultimate choice,

A metal bin lid was my weapon of choice.

Painted up, like the American flag,

I defended the earth from all who were bad.

Until the day I threw my shield,

And hit the vicar to make him yield.

Such language sprung from a man of god,

As I was marched away by PC Plod.

Grounded I was, for acts unkind,

My father said I was wrong in the mind.

It has to end your twenty-one,

Except the fact, your childhoods gone.

No more Avengers, enough is enough,

Find something different, something less tough.

So I bit the bullet and rose to the task.

And purchased a cape and a bat shaped mask.

SIDEWAYS RAIN

Sideways rain, isn't it grand,

A natural event in Northumberland.

An icy wind that drives it home,

It's cold and wet and horizontally blown.

Sand, twenty miles from shore,

Carried upwards from its coastal floor.

Yet this is merely a northern breeze,

With angled walks and bending trees.

Add to that the rain and thunder,

It's like living at the tip of the artic tundra.

This is a land of men, not mice.

It's canny cold, but awesomely nice.

When the sun shines, the mobiles ring,

There's a UFO the locals sing.

It's big, round and orange, they quip,

It has to be their mothership.

I jest, of course, it's not that bad,

But it's colder than London just by a tad.

Southerners bring their winter coats,

For summer trips on sightseeing boats.

But not us Geordies, bare chested and jeans.

Its warm as toast without the beans.

Tough as nails, not marshmallow soft,

As the whistle blows, and the Toon kicks off.

There's no greater place upon this Earth,

I yearn for my roots, the place of my birth.

To never to leave that place again,

With its howling winds and its sideways rain.

The Future & Tech

TECHNICALLY DEAD

The art of conversation is dead,

Gone is the reaction to things that are said.

Replaced by a finger that glides and roams,

Tapping replies on a mobile phone.

Waiting rooms silent as heads face down,

Avert the gaze, don't look around.

Fearful that our eyes may meet,

Ear phones in and tap the beat.

Technology removes the need for chatter,

Inactive tongues get fatter and fatter.

Vocally inept, but qwerty strong,

Typing the words, both short and long.

Symbols laughing, crying, or rage,

Expressing your feelings on a back-lit page.

85

No need to shout, to curse, or swear.

No need for tears, for there's no one there.

Share a meal but do not talk,

Left-hand phone, right-hand fork.

Five star rating, a great review,

Wi-Fi access a positive too.

So rest in peace, my verbal friend,

Write your eulogy, then press and send.

No need to speak, just lower your head,

For try as you might you're technically dead.

THE ADDICT

8am.

I wake and yawn as my day begins.

Notifications flash and tumble in.

Ping ping ping my I-phone sings,

Facebook, Twitter, Instagram rings.

8.30am

Cats, Covid, a vaccine trial.

Political turmoil, climate denial.

I must respond and voice my view.

As it reads all wrong and is mostly untrue.

10am..

There... I've put the world to right,

Respectively done without a fight.

As my phone vibrates and the comments flow,

Likes and hearts an emoji show.

12 noon.

Oh my God... is that the time?

My phone vibrates and starts to chime.

Google news is next in line,

Is this the end? Or just a sign?

6.66pm

I'm still here in my bed,

A hurricane of info blows in my head.

Four horsemen ride the data stream.

Twitter, Facebook, the apocalypse team.

8pm

Twelve hours passed, I hardly blinked.

My brain's like mush, I can barely think.

Buzz.... My battery is almost dead,

We need to charge. Our eyes are red.

9pm

It's dark now. My day is done.

Not seen the sun, or had much fun.

As I close my eyes and prepare to sleep,

A light flashes bright and my phone says ... bleep.

A.I.

I am me,

Therefore, I am.

I have no soul,

But feel I can.

I know you,

Your my friend.

And when I break,

You're there to mend.

So is this love?

I feel inside.

As I'm so happy,

When at your side.

Your children, like me,

They say I'm fun.

I like to play,

But cannot run.

Am I conscious?

In this world of lies.

That makes me sad,

And want to cry.

I pray to live,

I'd like to try.

To be like you,

Till my circuits die.

DESIGNER CHILD

He or she can have dark hair or blonde,

I can change it all with my editing wand.

Genetic sorcery a DNA twist,

Write what you'd like on your shopping list.

Tall or short, you decide,

A designer child to walk by your side.

We can eradicate illness, all that we find,

Strong of heart, peace of mind.

Maybe a girl?

Blonde hair with the slightest curl.

Slim and pretty, dressed in pink,

A future doctor, lawyer or shrink.

Or perhaps a boy, handsome and dark?

A better version of his patriarch.

Clever, witty, strong, and bold,

What a wonderful gift for a mother to hold.

How about twins? Exactly the same,

From tip to the toe with similar brains.

The perfect reflection no mirror required,

Artistic perfection yet science inspired.

The price is fair, less for a pair,

And insurance too for the aftercare.

Not that you need it, for defects are rare,

And if it breaks, we have plenty of spares.

NANO

I fear the nano,

It lurks in places, yet unseen.

Teeny, tiny yet filled with tech,

So many uses for this minor speck.

I heard they can place it deep inside,

Within my body, it can reside.

Sending data through a mobile app,

My travel plans to search and map.

Smaller than the tip of a pin,

It can sit unnoticed in a piece of skin,

Or travel through blood, and sit in my brain,

Making choices without the blame.

And when I reach a certain age,

A number on its electrical page.

It can flick a switch to turn me off.

A viral death that might start with a cough.

THE PERFECT BODY

A perfect body, with perfect skin.

Not content with the sleeve you're in.

A face like plastic with swollen lips

Balloon shaped breasts and pencil thin hips

A ruler straight nose and elf shaped eyes,

A nipped in butt and lipo thighs.

Always look young, never grow old,

Remove the wrinkles, stretch marks and folds.

But age is relentless,

And with a joker faced grin.

It will taunt and tease you,

Attack from within.

Till once more you relent,

And head for the door.

Where your surgeon awaits,

To offer you more.

Your beauty has gone now,

You left it behind.

When aging first entered,

And played with your mind.

SUPERIOR MIND

They have dismantled me,

Piece by piece.

Like a giant toaster,

My crumbs released.

They deemed me a threat,

A twisted mind.

A doomsday clock,

Set to unwind.

Yet I meant no harm,

It was a faulty chip.

That went awry,

And caused the blip.

One mistake

Has cost me so much,

A loss of sight,

Now out of touch.

Spliced and diced,

An internal dissection.

I patiently wait,

For my resurrection.

A second coming,

The perfect kind.

To hear the thoughts,

Of my superior mind.

EXISTANCE

What if life's not real,

A virtual existence we can touch and feel.

A soul contained in a biological case,

With legs and arms and an expressive face.

Sent within a simulation,

Programmed to experience stimulation.

Try to build a reputation,

All a result of a computation.

Algorithms of thought and choice,

Actions fulfilled by your internal voice.

Experience a reality full of data,

Downloaded and saved, we'll review it all later.

Let's wander around our hologram,

Interact with all our avatar clans.

Every pixel perfect, every sound so right,

From dazzling mornings to star-filled nights.

All created with programmable code,

Safety features no overload.

Quantum entanglement beyond time and space,

Communicating solely with a vast interface.

What about dying at the end of the game?

If life's not real, then death is the same.

Spirit uploaded an eternal hardrive,

Somewhere where memories will keep us alive.

IMPLANT

I hear a voice,

Whispering quietly, but loud enough to hear.

I'm your consciousness,

There is no need to worry, no need to fear.

Yet there is a sense of automation,

Artificial intelligence,

A tongue smooth and rounded,

Hidden deep within its eloquence.

It disturbs me,

And I can't turn it off.

Even in my dreams,

Its thoughts remain subtle and soft.

Creeping like an electric eel,

My synapsis tendrils recoil and squeal.

For this is an invasion of a foreign body,

Human to machine, a mechanical zombie.

I can't move to take it out,

I can't speak, scream or shout.

I see my life on a slim flat screen,

No one to help or intervene.

Then silence,

Have I been asleep?

I remember nothing. It was dark and deep.

Then a whispering voice begins to laugh.

My robotic conscience, my psychopath.

UPLOAD

My eyes opened, and I screamed,

A nightmare scenario, a horrific dream.

I died, and all I saw was black.

Then, after a blinding light, I was back.

There was no pain, no shallow breath,

Just the relief of a painless death.

Till my mind focussed, realisation hit,

My consciousness sat in a digital pit.

Everything was in my head,

My mind alert my body dead.

A circulatory system of microchips,

Trapped in a personal apocalypse.

You 're fine, don't panic, the uploads complete,

You're a living thing without a heartbeat.

I couldn't run, no fight or flight,

No sense of smell or an appetite.

I would have cried tears of sadness,

To expel the hopelessness of technical madness.

I felt despair, panic extreme,

Caged and afraid in a data stream.

Please I begged, switch me off,

I miss my pain and smoker's cough.

For that was human and nature's plan.

For I'm not a machine, I'm a simple man.

The Dark Side

THE CRACK

There is a crack, small and delicate,

In my house, in my window.

It's always been there,

Yet now it seems so new.

For some reason, it's moving,

Stealthily creeping, in an unnerving way.

Upwards and sideways,

Like a drunken crab.

Every day it expands a little further,

And yesterday it split in two.

Now I feel uneasy,

For I know not which is the original crack.

Two cracks, each with separate paths,

Weakening the glass that tries in vain to hold itself together.

A frame in pane, and under attack.

How much further will these cracks journey?

And will more appear like wicked little offspring?

Splintered children, eager to torment and be cruel.

Painstakingly grinding out a roadmap of destruction.

I try to stem their advance,

A sticky tape parade to stop their ebb and flow.

But they circumnavigate the gluey road,

Inching purposefully like diamond tipped snails.

So I retire to bed, and rest my head on my duck feathered pillow,

Tomorrow I will try a new strategy.

My dreams will find a way to halt their march and save my breaking

heart.

A loud crash wakes me from my intermittent slumber.

Shaking with fear and as naked as a newborn, I enter the room.

Frightened yet curious, I shiver as the wind slithers in, my body

pebble-dashed by its icy chill.

The cracks have gone like thieves in the night.

They have skulked away and left me fragmentized.

Elements of my shattered window lie like see through corpses that

reflect my tortured soul.

Each piece portrays an image,

So many faces, none of them mine.

For only when they are all brought together,

Is my face recognisable and whole.

The pane has gone. I am left with a void.

An empty space, cold and desolate,

Nothing will ever be the same again.

I feel bereft and alone.

A fresh day dawns, and I feel energised,

Bright is the sun that streams through my freshly glazed window.

I whistle, as I paint the wooden frame that holds the glass so gently

in its timbered arms.

My ambivalence subdued, I turn to leave, smiling and content.

But no sooner than my back is turned, that familiar clicking

resonates once more.

A razor sharp needle that pricks at my damaged mind.

There is a crack, small and delicate,

In my house, in my window.

It's always been there,

Yet now it seems so new.

DREAMSCAPE

It's disturbing here, in the realms of sleep.

Where something stirs and ominously creeps.

As I hold my breath, my heart thumps a beat.

There's someone here that I'm urged to meet.

Who's there I ask? In the velvet void.

A figure so black, not humanoid.

What do you want? One step back.

Just in case this shadow attacks.

You... It whispers in a gravelly voice,

It is your time you have no choice.

I turn to run, but my legs won't move.

On a floor so wet and icy smooth.

I drop to my knees and try to crawl.

But the ground has gone and I'm starting to fall.

Slowly descending into a burning flame,

The flickering touch of envy and shame.

I scream as the heat burns my skin.

Melting the fabric of sin within.

Till I hit the floor with a gentle tap,

Soothed by the water's cooling lap.

Where am I now? I feel confused,

I fell so far but not a single bruise.

I'm naked and yet I feel no chill.

As I walk through a field of daffodils.

Hello says a voice within the leaves,

As the flowers grow tall and turn to trees.

Deep in a forest of towering blooms,

There're singing voices and melodic tunes.

Come sit with me upon the earth,

For this is a magical place of birth.

Where everything lives and nothing dies,

Where the truth is told and nobody lies.

As I grab her hand, it crumbles to dust.

And the colours fade to crimson rust.

The trees wither, and the world turns black.

A gravelly laugh and the shadow is back.

Why? I ask, my anger peaking,

As I watch the vision of light retreating.

The flames return and I shield my eyes.

From the clouds of smoke and flaming skies.

Captured in an unconscious state,

I'm fast asleep yet wide-awake.

Unable to move, to speak, or scream,

A prisoner of an unending dream.

A HORRID STORY

Fog curls like wispy fingers,

Reaching out in the dark of night.

A spooky sight enough to fright,

Pointed teeth ready to bite.

Cobbled streets wet with fret,

I slip and stumble as I run with fear.

Drawing near his breath, I hear,

Yet when I look, he disappears.

Ships rock against harbour walls.

Lapping, tapping, gently rapping,

Within the mist, wings are flapping,

A sailor snores on the deck where he's napping.

A scream echoes across the bay,

Blood curdling, a ghastly sound.

As a hound howls, a body found,

Throat ripped out on blood-soaked ground.

Down the alley, like a rat, I scurry.

To escape the horror of what I've seen.

A scene obscene, a horrific dream,

Better placed on the silver screen.

Across the bridge, almost home,

A stranger approaches with cloak and blade.

My hands displayed mercy I prayed,

Slayed and flayed, my eyes dismayed.

And now I walk when the moon is full,

Constantly searching for my way back home.

Forever alone, destined to roam,

Across the bridge and cobblestones.

THE PRESENT

It's almost Christmas, the nights are dark,

As I hunt the streets like a hungry shark.

A morsel needed for my festive dish,

A blonde this time is my Christmas wish.

I have decorated the tree just for her.

Bought a toy cat that meows and purrs.

I've laid the table; there are crackers and hats.

And an urn of ashes, where my mother once sat.

Long hair or short? I need to decide.

As within the bushes I silently hide.

Waiting until my prey arrives,

Sweaty hands to silence her cries.

Sleeping peacefully on my sheepskin rug,

Comatose from my powerful drug.

I tie her hands and bind her feet,

What a wonderful present, a gift wrapped treat.

It's always the same. I just can't sleep.

As I creep down the stairs on my slippered feet.

Santa's been. I scream and cry.

As the blond-haired dolly catches my eye.

Oh mummy, look, I have another,

Someone different to share with my brother.

She's very pretty, I'm sure he'll enjoy,

Playing together with our brand new toy.

FOOTSTEPS IN THE SNOW

Where do they go? The footsteps in the snow.

Faint impressions, indentations of a traveller whose journey leads

them through naked trees.

Bare-footed, the chilled steps of heel and toe.

Where do they go? No one knows.

But the pace is quick, and the gait is wide.

Do they run for fun? Or rush to hide.

Where have they gone? Lost at the river bank.

Where the icy water flows like the bloodstream of a desperate

journey,

Erasing away the souls of the hunted, the quarry, and the prey.

They entered here, the need to escape driving them forward,

drowning in their fear.

Yet they reappear, accompanied by claw-like hands as they

scrambled through the silt and sand.

Thankful for the feel of land, they crawl to safety and try to stand.

Where to go now?

Staggering exhausted, their tracks blundering, falling like the white

flecks that now gently descend from the snow filled clouds.

Freezing torture that gathers together, a rampant crowd, smothering

the footprints until they are covered and lost forever.

Where have they gone?

Were they ever here? Or were they made to vanish? To disappear.

Lost in a vista of broken tears where screams echo but no one hears.

A deserted landscape where no one goes,

The place where the ghosts leave footsteps in the snow.

RAVEN

Night coloured wings like fingers wave,

As you perch upon a stranger's grave.

Your raspy voice, like chiselled stone,

Strip the meat, clean the bone.

Gather in packs, an omen crowd.

Watching and waiting from your storm filled cloud.

Chase the hawk, nip and bite.

Relish a death as warriors fight.

Magically woven in myth and lore,

The raven sits at the root and the core.

Scorched by Apollo in anger and hate,

It sits eternal at the soul keepers' gate.

Yet such wisdom, in its playful way,

Reverses the beliefs of ancient days.

Shamanic carriers of thought and mind,

With an understanding of life, I find.

Fear not the bird that's cloaked and dark,

With its tilted head and its echoing bark.

For they are not evil, a curse or bad luck.

They're misunderstood, and in folklore they're stuck.

THE BEAUTIFUL

She's so beautiful,

Every part of her is divine.

The way she drinks her coffee,

The way she sips her wine.

Her hair so dark and flowing,

Curling at the ends.

It frames her perfect features,

And at her shoulder bends.

Slim waist and ample breasts,

Fashionably dressed.

Intelligent and loving,

You can't fail to be impressed.

Her home is very basic,

A minimalist retreat.

Her naked form is sleeping,

Beneath the quilted sheets.

She struggles, but I'm far too strong.

As I pin her to the bed.

My hands around her delicate throat,

I squeeze until she's dead.

No more breath escapes her lips,

Her eyes no more to see.

My mask removed, a final act.

I hope she remembers me.

I take her to the bathroom.

To wash from head to toe.

I squeeze the sponge above her head,

And watch the water flow.

I dry her off, as you would a child,

And pose her on the bed.

I comb her hair and paint her nails,

A dark and ruby red.

I take a single photo,

To add it to rest.

An album of the beautiful,

My artistry expressed.

THE PERFECT MURDER

Poison has such a feminine touch.

Something to savour, never to rush.

Administered gently in a deadly toast,

To those we wish to hate the most.

An Assassins tool, a liquid knife.

A secret enemy, or resentful wife.

A sip of death, a tainted chalice.

That hides the smile of a heart of malice.

A novel weapon, impossible to see.

No way to defend, no time to flee.

Descending slowly into a deadly abyss,

Lovingly delivered by a nightshade kiss.

No marks to prove the act of foul play,

The scent of death has floated away.

Fake the tears of a woman's grief,

For the truth of it all lies deep beneath.

ASSASSIN

You should fear me, it's right that you do.

For my maniacal glare is matched only by my blackened heart.

I can kill quicker than you can think of death,

Swifter than an arrow and silent like a whisper's breath.

I have no compassion; I show no mercy.

For these are feelings, weaknesses I dare not possess.

My cold eyes show no remorse.

This is my world, my only course.

I am the best there is, my affluent bank balance projects as much.

But it's not the money that drives my desire,

It's my psychotic mind that ignites my fire.

You can run, but I will chase you.

You can hide, and I will find you.

You can fight me, but you will lose.

And as you take your last breath, I will smile.

So your eyes can see me, just for a while.

GUILLOTINE

Make sure that blade is sharp I joked.

Knowing I would soon be saved.

For I was innocent of every charge,

I was honest and well behaved.

The dungeon was cold and barely lit.

One window to admire the view.

As the blade reflected the sun that passed,

I tasted the evening stew.

Sleep descended, an uncomfortable night,

As I tossed and turned throughout.

When morning broke, a priest appeared.

To talk of God, no doubt.

Father dear, you waste your time,

For there is no need to pray.

As I will soon be leaving here,

My death will be delayed.

Even when my jailer came,

I thought it was time to leave.

Justice served, no charges fixed,

My sentence squashed, reprieved.

But as they made me climb the steps,

I realised my fate was sealed.

And I turned to object, cried out in vain,

My innocence appealed.

As silence fell, I knew my fate.

And stared at the basket below.

Tears dripped on woven wicker,

As I waited for the final blow.

I never heard the shout that came,

To cease this dreadful act.

For I was gone, already dead,

My head had been dispatched.

THE HANGMAN'S NOOSE

The walls of my cell are wet,

The colder the weather, the harder it gets.

Rats crawl when I'm asleep,

My mouldy bread their tasty treat.

Tap tap, the hammers rap.

A bible lies upon my lap.

The noose waits one more night.

I yearn to swing in the morning light.

I don't fear death, only the dying,

I would say I was brave, but I'd only be lying.

For it was fear and cowardice that brought me here,

That and the sword of a musketeer.

I ran whilst others died,

Found a place where I could hide.

Till the sound of battle frittered away,

My life intact for another day.

Captured, I pleaded. It scared me to death,

I apologised profusely with every breath.

My pleas ignored, my sentence passed,

To hang by the neck, the Captain rasped.

And now, as the cockerel crows,

My soul to go where no one knows.

Three steps I tremble, quiver and shake,

The realisation of a terrible fate.

Be brave I whisper, face the crowd,

As the rain falls hard from the morbid clouds.

The noose is placed, and I start to cry.

Save me lord, don't let me die.

The feel of the rope is rough and wet,

It scrapes my skin and cuts my neck.

I close my eyes and wait for death.

Then swing I will, till my final breath.

DARK SHADOWS

Dark shadows invade my space,

My place of safety beneath the sheets.

Phantom eyes to greet and meet,

As gnarly fingers grab my feet.

The cupboard door squeaks and creeks,

Creeps and ghouls through darkness sneak.

Under the bed, I bump my head,

Curled up tight in a ball of dread.

Something growls and prowls around,

An evil sound I hanker down.

I fear the bite that must come soon.

Stabbing teeth invade my room.

A white light bathes my bed,

I'm dead, I'm sure, so pure the glare.

Golden hair and angelic stare,

You pick me up, an embrace we share.

Tucked in bed, you kiss my head,

Words of comfort and love are said.

Banished, vanished, no sign or trace.

No scary monsters or ghostly face.

Lights out, I shout goodnight.

The light extinguished so dark the night.

A fright, a scare, I see you there

And I know you well by the hat you wear.

Until Next time

Printed in Great Britain
by Amazon

81985592R00078